BACK TO YOUR
ROOTS!

BACK TO YOUR ROOTS!

DELICIOUS ROOT VEGETABLE RECIPES

This edition published by Parragon Books Ltd in 2014
LOVE FOOD is an imprint of Parragon Books Ltd

Parragon Books Ltd
Chartist House
15–17 Trim Street
Bath BA1 1HA, UK
www.parragon.com/lovefood

ISBN 978-1-4723-2983-7

Printed in China

New recipes written by Sarah Bush
Introduction and incidental text by Christine McFadden
New photography by Mike Cooper
New home economy by Lincoln Jefferson
Additional design work by Geoff Borin
Internal illustrations by Julie Ingham and Nicola O'Byrne

Notes for the Reader
This book uses both metric and imperial measurements. Follow the same units of measurement throughout; do not mix metric and imperial. All spoon measurements are level: teaspoons are assumed to be 5 ml, and tablespoons are assumed to be 15 ml. Unless otherwise stated, milk is assumed to be full fat, eggs and individual vegetables are medium, and pepper is freshly ground black pepper. Unless otherwise stated, all root vegetables should be peeled prior to using.

Garnishes, decorations and serving suggestions are all optional and not necessarily included in the recipe ingredients or method. The times given are an approximate guide only. Preparation times differ according to the techniques used by different people and the cooking times may also vary from those given. Optional ingredients, variations or serving suggestions have not been included in the time calculations.

Picture acknowledgements
The publisher would like to thank the following for the permission to reproduce copyright material: Cover illustrations courtesy of iStock; page 13: Different vegetables in a crate © Beyond fotomedia/Junos; page 75: Still life of carrots and beets in a colander © Aurora Open/Justin Baille; page 112: Organic assorted beets © The Agency Collection/Mint Images/Tim Pannell; page 113: Radishes © Image Source.

CONTENTS

LET'S GET TO THE ROOT OF THE MATTER!

We tend to think of root vegetables as homely comfort foods, but these buried treasures have surprisingly feisty flavours, and come in an artist's palette of colours. Botanically speaking, they are not all roots. Some are tubers – the swollen tips of underground stems. These include potatoes, yams and Jerusalem artichokes, whereas beetroot, carrots and radishes are straightforward roots.

BEETROOT
Beetroot comes in familiar garnet red, plus golden yellow, white and stunning pink and white candy stripes. Its slightly odd flavour is sweet and earthy with a little background bitterness. It goes well with horseradish, buttermilk, juniper and dill.

CELERIAC
With its pock-marked skin and hairy tangle of roots, celeriac is not the most beautiful of vegetables, but the flavour more than makes up for its looks. It's the root to go for when you want the freshness of celery along with the starchy comfort of potato.

CARROT
Not only do carrots help you see in the dark, they come in an assortment of shapes, sizes and colours and not just regulation orange. There are yellow, red, purple and white varieties too. Raw or cooked they look stunning on the plate.

JERUSALEM ARTICHOKE
These elongated tubers are an undistinguished beige, though some are a more striking reddish-pink. They have a unique, earthy, nutty flavour, similar to globe artichokes.

PARSNIP

A quietly understated vegetable, parsnips may be slim and tapering, or wide-shouldered heavyweights. The ivory flesh is clean-tasting and sweet without being cloying.

POTATO

Potatoes range from monster bakers to pebble-sized earlies. The skin may be familiar beige, rosy pink or red, or sometimes blue or purple, with ivory, buttery yellow or even sumptuous swirling purple flesh. Textures also vary. Some are floury and perfect for mashing, others are creamy, and there are waxy ones that are lovely in salads.

RADISH

Radishes span a spectrum of sizes, shapes and colours. There are small, mild red-skinned varieties, large rough-and-ready black-skinned ones, and exotic types with luminous green or raspberry-red flesh. They all have a crisp juicy texture with a peppery flavour that varies in intensity.

SWEDE

Recognizable by the two-tone skin – purple on top and a dusky yellow below – the swede is a rugged root with dense golden flesh and a sinus-clearing peppery flavour. It is delicious mashed, roasted or fried, or even grated raw in salads.

SWEET POTATO

The most common of these torpedo-shaped tubers have thick, brownish-orange skin with vivid orange, moist, sweet flesh. They are good roasted, mashed or baked, and also work well in sweet dishes, especially tarts and pies.

TURNIP

Related to the swede and radish, turnips vary in shape – some are flat like spinning tops, others are round or elongated. The flesh is less dense than swede with a sweeter, mellower flavour.

YAM

Relatively new to the supermarkets, the yam is a versatile tropical tuber with a rough brown skin and sticky creamy-white flesh. It can be boiled, baked, fried or mashed just like potatoes.

FEEL THE BENEFIT

There's no question about the strong link between good health and a diet rich in vegetables. Together with fruit, vegetables feature in the nutritional guidelines of all major countries, and experts universally agree that eating more of them may help protect against chronic and life-threatening diseases, such as heart disease and cancer.

Vegetables not only provide vitamins, minerals and fibre, they also contain antioxidants, a nutrient group that protects the body by deactivating substances known as free radicals. It's believed that they attack DNA, the genetic material in the nucleus of a cell, and the resulting changes may cause cancer. Free radicals also cause oxidative damage linked to premature ageing, cataracts and hardening of the arteries.

Though often overlooked, root vegetables have excellent nutritional credentials. They all contain slow-release carbohydrate that makes you feel full and keeps your energy levels stable. Most have a desirably low glycaemic index score, the exceptions being potatoes and parsnips. You can substitute sweet potato for these if you are tracking your GI score.

Roots are packed with health-promoting fibre, both the cholesterol-lowering soluble kind, and the insoluble type that used to be called 'roughage' – the most helpful for dealing with constipation. Super-fibrous types – old carrots and parsnips, for example – also contain a woody

substance called lignin, found in the core. It's thought to lower blood cholesterol levels and therefore the risk of clogged-up arteries.

Some root vegetables have special properties. Beetroot, for example, contains a group of colour pigments known as betalains. These have antioxidant and anti-inflammatory properties but also trigger enzymes that bind together harmful substances in the cells and make them more easily excreted from the body.

As the name suggests, carrots are rich in carotenoids, as are orange-fleshed sweet potatoes. Carotenoids include not just the better-known beta-carotene, which is converted to vitamin A in the body, but alpha-carotene and lutein too, valued for their cancer-fighting properties. A daily carrot is also believed to improve night vision.

THE ULTIMATE IN COMFORT

VEG OUT!

Root vegetables are relatively cheap and have a reasonable shelf life, so there are plenty of places to buy them.

IN THE CITY

Large supermarkets are an obvious choice, but there are other options. Shops selling African or Asian vegetables are a treasure trove. You'll find yams, sweet potatoes and a host of root vegetables that you may never have set eyes on before. They are all worth a try. And let's not forget the traditional greengrocer. Many have closed down but the survivors often have an excellent choice. Bear in mind that root vegetables do not do well in an overheated, brightly lit environment, so avoid newsagents and petrol stations.

IN THE COUNTRY

For freshness and seasonality it's hard to beat a good farm shop. The vegetables are likely to have been grown on the farm, or within a defined radius. Buying direct from the farm also reduces food miles, though this is a double-edged sword if you think of the miles involved getting to and from the farm. There is certainly less waste. Farmers sell vegetables regardless of cosmetic irregularities, and without unnecessary packaging to dispose of when you get home.

IN A BOX

If you are pressed for time, an alternative is the vegetable box scheme. Subscribers regularly receive a box containing whatever vegetables are in season. You can usually choose the size of box to suit your lifestyle, or veto a vegetable if you don't like it. Invariably you will need to use your imagination to come up with different ways of cooking the same vegetable, particularly if it has a long season.

BUYING ORGANIC

Root vegetables absorb herbicides, pesticides and fungicides that end up in the soil, so you may want to consider buying organic ones, especially if you eat a particular type every day. They are more expensive but generally come out with flying colours in taste trials. You'll find organic vegetables in good supermarkets, but they are likely to have clocked up food miles. You may do better to try a good health food shop or an organic farm or market garden if there is one near you.

CELERIAC SOUP WITH CHEESE PASTRY STICKS

SERVES: 4　　　　**PREP TIME: 15 MINS**　　　　**COOK TIME: 45 MINS**

INGREDIENTS

3 tbsp olive oil
1 onion, chopped
1 celeriac, cut into chunks
1 litre/1¾ pints vegetable stock
1 small bunch fresh thyme, chopped
salt and pepper
fresh thyme sprigs, to garnish

CHEESE STICKS

375 g/13 oz ready-made puff pastry, thawed if frozen
plain flour, for dusting
1 egg, beaten
100 g/3½ oz finely grated Parmesan cheese
butter, for greasing
pepper

1. Heat the oil in a large saucepan over a medium heat, add the onion and cook, stirring frequently, for 4–5 minutes, until soft but not coloured.

2. Add the celeriac and cook, stirring frequently, for 3–4 minutes. Pour in the stock and add the thyme. Simmer for 25 minutes, or until the celeriac is tender. Meanwhile, preheat the oven to 200°C/400°F/Gas Mark 6.

3. To make the cheese sticks, thinly roll out the pastry on a floured work surface. Brush with half the egg, scatter over half the cheese and season well with pepper.

4. Fold the pastry in half. Brush with the remaining egg, scatter with the remaining cheese and season with pepper. Lightly grease and line two baking sheets.

5. Cut the pastry into strips about 1 cm/½ inch wide. Twist gently along their length to produce spirals. Place on the prepared baking sheets and bake in the preheated oven for 5 minutes, or until crisp and golden.

6. Purée the soup in the pan using a hand-held blender and gently reheat. Season to taste with salt and pepper. Ladle the soup into warmed bowls, garnish with thyme sprigs and serve with the warm pastry sticks.

SWEET POTATO & APPLE SOUP

SERVES: 6 **PREP TIME: 15 MINS** **COOK TIME: 45 MINS**

INGREDIENTS

1 tbsp butter
3 leeks, thinly sliced
1 large carrot, thinly sliced
600 g/1 lb 5 oz sweet potatoes, diced
2 large Bramley apples, peeled, cored and diced
1.2 litres/2 pints water
freshly grated nutmeg
225 ml/8 fl oz apple juice
225 ml/8 fl oz single cream
salt and pepper
snipped fresh chives or coriander, to garnish

1. Melt the butter in a large saucepan over a medium–low heat.

2. Add the leeks, cover and cook for 6–8 minutes, or until soft, stirring frequently.

3. Add the carrot, sweet potatoes, apples and water. Lightly season to taste with salt, pepper and nutmeg. Bring to the boil, reduce the heat and simmer, covered, for about 20 minutes, stirring occasionally, until the vegetables are very tender.

4. Leave the soup to cool slightly, then purée in the pan with a hand-held blender.

5. Stir in the apple juice, place over a low heat and simmer for about 10 minutes, until heated through.

6. Stir in the cream and simmer for a further 5 minutes, stirring frequently, until heated through. Taste and adjust the seasoning, if necessary.

7. Ladle the soup into warmed bowls, garnish with chives and serve.

HERO TIPS

This soup is great for using up any excess apples you may have after a good apple season. You can also garnish the soup with thin eating apple slices.

JERUSALEM ARTICHOKE SOUP

SERVES: 4-6   **PREP TIME: 15 MINS**   **COOK TIME: 45 MINS**

INGREDIENTS

55 g/2 oz butter

2 onions, chopped

675 g/1 lb 8 oz Jerusalem artichokes, sliced and dropped into water to prevent discoloration

850 ml/1½ pints vegetable stock

300 ml/10 fl oz milk

salt and pepper

CROÛTONS

4 tbsp vegetable oil

2 slices of day-old white bread, crusts removed, bread cut into 1-cm/½-inch cubes

1. To make the croûtons, heat the oil in a frying pan over a medium heat. Add the croûtons in a single layer and fry, tossing occasionally, until golden brown and crisp.

2. Remove the pan from the heat and transfer the croûtons to kitchen paper to drain.

3. Melt the butter in a large saucepan over a medium heat. Add the onions and cook until soft.

4. Add the drained artichokes and mix well with the butter. Cover the pan and cook slowly over a low heat for about 10 minutes.

5. Pour in the stock, bring to the boil, then reduce the heat and simmer, covered, for 20 minutes.

6. Remove from the heat and leave to cool slightly. Blend in the saucepan using a hand-held blender. Stir in the milk, season to taste with salt and pepper, then return the soup to the heat and heat until hot.

7. Ladle the soup into warmed bowls, sprinkle over the croûtons and serve immediately.

HERO TIPS

It is important to leave the soup to cool quite a bit before blending to avoid getting any hot splashes from the soup during processing.

ROAST ROOT SOUP WITH GINGER

SERVES: 4-6　　　　**PREP TIME: 20 MINS**　　**COOK TIME: 45 MINS**

INGREDIENTS

1 onion
½ small swede
1 sweet potato
2 carrots
1 potato
5 tbsp olive oil
2 tbsp tomato purée
¼ tsp pepper
2 large garlic cloves, peeled
2 tbsp groundnut oil
2 x 5-cm/2-inch pieces fresh ginger, sliced into thin shreds
850 ml/1½ pints hot vegetable stock
½ tsp sea salt
crème fraîche and roughly chopped fresh flat-leaf parsley, to garnish

1. Preheat the oven to 190°C/375°F/Gas Mark 5. Peel the onion, swede, sweet potato, carrots and potato and cut into large, even-sized chunks.

2. Mix the olive oil, tomato purée and pepper in a large bowl. Add the vegetables and the garlic and toss to coat.

3. Spread out the vegetables in a roasting tray. Roast in the preheated oven for 20 minutes, or until the garlic is soft. Remove the garlic and set aside. Roast the vegetables for a further 10–15 minutes, until tender.

4. Meanwhile, heat the groundnut oil in a frying pan over a high heat. Add the ginger and fry, turning constantly, for 1–2 minutes, until crisp. Immediately remove the ginger from the pan and drain on kitchen paper. Set aside and keep warm.

5. Put the garlic and the other roasted vegetables into a food processor. Process to a rough purée.

6. Pour the purée into a saucepan and add the stock. Add the salt, then simmer, stirring, for 1–2 minutes, until heated through.

7. Ladle the soup into warmed serving bowls and swirl in a little crème fraîche. Top with the sizzled ginger threads and chopped parsley and serve immediately.

BEETROOT BORSCHT SOUP

Borscht is a soup that originates from the Ukraine. It has become popular across the world due to emigrants from Eastern Europe taking the recipe with them to Western Europe and the USA.

SERVES: 6   **PREP TIME: 15 MINS**   **COOK TIME: 1¼ HRS**

INGREDIENTS

1 onion

55 g/2 oz butter

350 g/12 oz raw beetroots, cut into thin batons, and 1 raw beetroot, grated

1 carrot, cut into thin batons

3 celery sticks, thinly sliced

2 tomatoes, peeled, deseeded and chopped

1.4 litres/2½ pints vegetable stock

1 tbsp white wine vinegar

1 tbsp sugar

2 tbsp snipped fresh dill

115 g/4 oz white cabbage, shredded

150 ml/5 fl oz soured cream

salt and pepper

crusty bread, to serve

1. Slice the onion into rings. Melt the butter in a large heavy-based saucepan. Add the onion and cook over a low heat, stirring occasionally, for 3–5 minutes, or until softened. Add the beetroot batons, carrot, celery and tomatoes and cook, stirring frequently, for 4–5 minutes.

2. Add the stock, vinegar, sugar and 1 tablespoon of the dill into the saucepan. Season to taste with salt and pepper. Bring to the boil, reduce the heat and simmer for 35–40 minutes, or until the vegetables are tender.

3. Stir in the cabbage, cover and simmer for 10 minutes. Stir in the grated beetroot, with any juices, and cook for a further 10 minutes. Ladle into warmed bowls. Top with the soured cream, sprinkle with the remaining dill and serve with crusty bread.

HERO TIPS

Beetroot is rich in the compounds that safeguard our health – it is high in several important vitamins and minerals and contains antioxidants.

POTATO & SWEETCORN FRITTERS WITH RELISH

SERVES: 8

PREP TIME: 20 MINS PLUS RESTING

COOK TIME: 20 MINS

INGREDIENTS

55 g/2 oz wholemeal flour
½ tsp ground coriander
½ tsp cumin seeds
¼ tsp chilli powder
½ tsp turmeric
¼ tsp salt
1 egg
3 tbsp milk
350 g/12 oz potatoes
1–2 garlic cloves, crushed
4 spring onions, chopped
55 g/2 oz sweetcorn kernels
vegetable oil, for shallow frying

ONION & TOMATO RELISH

1 onion
225 g/8 oz tomatoes
2 tbsp chopped fresh coriander
2 tbsp chopped fresh mint
2 tbsp lemon juice
½ tsp roasted cumin seeds
¼ tsp salt
pinch of cayenne pepper

1. To make the relish, cut the onion and tomatoes into small dice and place in a bowl with the remaining ingredients. Mix together well and leave to stand for at least 15 minutes before serving to allow the flavours to blend.

2. Place the flour in a bowl, stir in the spices and salt and make a well in the centre. Add the egg and milk and mix to form a fairly thick batter.

3. Coarsely grate the potatoes, place them in a sieve and rinse well under cold running water. Drain and squeeze dry, then stir them into the batter with the garlic, spring onions and sweetcorn and mix to combine thoroughly.

4. Heat about 5 mm/¼ inch of oil in a large frying pan and add a few tablespoons of the mixture at a time, flattening each to form a thin cake. Fry over a low heat, turning frequently, for 2–3 minutes, or until golden brown and cooked through.

5. Drain the fritters on kitchen paper and keep them hot while frying the remaining mixture in the same way. Serve the potato fritters hot with the relish.

CARROT & CORIANDER SAUSAGES & MASH

SERVES: 4

PREP TIME: 20 MINS PLUS CHILLING

COOK TIME: 30-35 MINS

INGREDIENTS
SAUSAGES

1 tbsp olive oil

25 g/1 oz spring onions, chopped

1 garlic clove, chopped

½ fresh red chilli, deseeded and finely chopped

1 tsp ground cumin

450 g/1 lb carrot, grated

½ tsp salt

3 tbsp crunchy peanut butter

25 g/1 oz finely chopped fresh coriander, plus extra to garnish

100 g/3½ oz fresh brown breadcrumbs

plain flour, for dusting

vegetable oil, for frying

MASH

900 g/2 lb floury potatoes, chopped

3 tbsp milk

55 g/2 oz margarine or butter

salt and pepper

1. To make the sausages, heat the olive oil in a large saucepan over a medium heat. Fry the spring onions, garlic, chilli and cumin for 2 minutes. Stir in the carrots and salt and mix well. Cover the pan and cook on a very low heat for 6–8 minutes, or until the carrot is tender.

2. Transfer the carrot mixture to a large mixing bowl and mix in the peanut butter and coriander, ensuring that the ingredients are thoroughly combined. Allow the mixture to cool, and then mix in the breadcrumbs.

3. On a floured surface, form the mixture into eight large sausages. Leave to chill in the refrigerator for up to an hour. Heat the vegetable oil in a frying pan over a medium heat and fry the sausages gently for 10 minutes, turning occasionally, until browned.

4. Meanwhile, bring a large saucepan of lightly salted water to the boil. Add the potatoes, bring back to the boil and cook for 15–20 minutes, or until cooked through and fluffy. Transfer to a mixing bowl, add the milk and margarine and mash the mixture thoroughly until all lumps are removed. Season to taste with salt and pepper.

5. Place the mashed potato on warmed plates and top with the sausages. Garnish with coriander and serve.

SWEET POTATO PANCAKES

MAKES: 4   **PREP TIME: 15 MINS**   **COOK TIME: 25 MINS**

INGREDIENTS

200 ml/7 fl oz milk

50 g/1¾ oz plain flour

50 g/1¾ oz chickpea (gram) flour

100 g/3½ oz sweet potato, grated

1 small red onion, finely chopped

vegetable oil, for frying

FILLING

150 g/5½ oz fresh baby spinach leaves, shredded

20 g/¾ oz currants

1 tbsp olive oil

30 g/1 oz pine nuts

salt and pepper

1. To make the filling, place the spinach in a saucepan over a medium heat. Add a splash of water and cook for about 2–3 minutes or until wilted. Turn out onto a plate, then blot firmly with kitchen paper to squeeze out as much water as possible. Set aside.

2. To make the pancakes, whisk together the milk, plain flour and chickpea flour in a large bowl. Stir in the sweet potato and onion, and mix thoroughly.

3. Heat a small amount of vegetable oil in a large frying pan over a high heat and pour a quarter of the pancake mixture into the pan, using the back of a spoon to spread the mixture out to the edges of the pan. Fry for 2–3 minutes on each side, turning carefully, until brown and crisp. Transfer to a warmed plate lined with kitchen paper and make three more pancakes.

4. Return the spinach to the saucepan with the currants, olive oil and pine nuts and place over a medium heat. Season with salt and pepper and cook for a minute or until heated through. Take a quarter of the spinach mixture and place on one half of a pancake. Fold over the other half. Repeat with the remaining pancakes and serve immediately while still warm.

GET FRESH!

When you shop for root vegetables be discerning, especially if buying from a market stall. There is no reason why you shouldn't choose the best on offer instead of taking what the stall-holder decides to select on your behalf.

Roots should feel firm and smell pleasantly fresh. Ideally, choose earth-encrusted ones; the soil acts as a protective barrier and keeps them in good condition. Once you get them home, shake off excess soil but resist the urge to wash it all off until you are ready to cook.

If buying plastic-wrapped roots from a supermarket, inspect carefully for signs of bruising and make sure the flesh feels firm through the plastic.

BEETROOT
Select: small-to-medium (large ones can be woody), leaves preferably attached, firm flesh.

Reject: spongy texture, bruises, cracks.

CARROT
Select: firm flesh, crisp when snapped.

Reject: greening round the top, cracks, whiskery rootlets, brown patches, slime, small holes (a sign of pest invasion).

CELERIAC
Select: slightly damp skin, firm flesh, heavy for size.

Reject: soft spots, bruises, brown patches.

JERUSALEM ARTICHOKE
Select: firm flesh, crisp when snapped.

Reject: spongy texture, bruises, broken or dry tips.

PARSNIP
Select: small-to-medium (large ones can be woody), firm flesh.

Reject: spongy texture, bruises, slime, cracks, sprouting at the top.

POTATO

Select: taut skin, firm flesh.

Reject: spongy texture, green patches, bruises, slime, cracks, sprouting eyes.

RADISH

Select: slightly damp skin, firm flesh, leaves preferably attached.

Reject: spongy texture, bruises, cracks, sprouting at the top.

SWEDE

Select: small-to-medium (large ones can be woody), firm flesh, heavy for size.

Reject: spongy texture, bruises, cracks.

SWEET POTATO

Select: taut skin, firm flesh.

Reject: spongy texture, bruises, cracks.

TURNIP

Select: small-to-medium (large ones can be woody), taut skin, firm flesh.

Reject: pitted skin, spongy texture, bruises.

YAM

Select: taught skin, firm flesh. If sold in sections, the cut end should be mould-free and sealed with clingfilm.

Reject: spongy texture, bruises, cracks, slime, mould.

YAM & BEEF STEW WITH COUSCOUS

SERVES: 4-6

PREP TIME: 15 MINS PLUS MARINATING

COOK TIME: 1½ HRS

INGREDIENTS

800 g/1 lb 12 oz stewing beef

2 onions, chopped

200 g/7 oz yams, cubed

200 g/7 oz new potatoes, halved

400 g/14 oz canned chickpeas, drained and rinsed

400 g/14 oz canned chopped tomatoes

200 ml/7 fl oz red wine or water

salt and pepper

MARINADE

2 tbsp vegetable oil

2 tbsp chopped fresh coriander

2 cinnamon sticks

1 tbsp clear honey

1 tsp ground paprika

1 tsp ground cumin

1 tsp harissa paste

1 tsp salt

COUSCOUS

200 g/7 oz couscous

1 tbsp roughly chopped fresh flat-leaf parsley

1 small bunch spring onions, trimmed and chopped

juice of 1 lemon

2 tbsp olive oil

1. Trim the beef, cut into 2.5-cm/1-inch pieces and put into a large bowl. Add the marinade ingredients and stir well to combine. Cover and chill in the refrigerator for 6 hours or overnight.

2. Preheat the oven to 190°C/375°F/Gas Mark 5. Transfer the meat and the marinade to a casserole dish and add the onions, yams, new potatoes and chickpeas. Pour over the tomatoes and wine and stir well. Cook in the preheated oven for 1 hour.

3. Remove from the oven, stir well and check the seasoning. If all the liquid has been absorbed add enough water to create a generous sauce. Return the casserole to the oven and cook for a further 30 minutes, or until the meat is tender.

4. Meanwhile, put the couscous into a bowl and pour over 250 ml/9 fl oz boiling water. Season to taste with salt and leave to stand for 5 minutes. Stir in the parsley and spring onions and drizzle over the lemon juice and olive oil. Remove the cinnamon sticks from the stew and serve immediately with the couscous.

BEETROOT BURGERS IN A BUN

These wholesome, crisp beetroot-and-millet burgers originally hail from Australia. The tangy yogurt sauce contrasts with the sweet, earthy flavour of the vegetables.

MAKES: 5

PREP TIME: 30 MINS PLUS CHILLING

COOK TIME: 35-40 MINS

INGREDIENTS

100 g/3½ oz millet (available in health food shops)

175 ml/6 fl oz lightly salted water

150 g/5½ oz raw beetroot, grated

30 g/1 oz carrots, grated

175 g/6 oz courgettes, grated

60 g/2¼ oz walnuts, finely chopped

2 tbsp cider vinegar

2 tbsp extra virgin olive oil, plus extra for frying

1 egg

2 tbsp cornflour

225 ml/8 fl oz natural yogurt

2 tsp finely chopped garlic

5 multi-grain buns, split

lettuce leaves

salt and pepper

1. Rinse and drain the millet and place in a small saucepan with the salted water. Place over a medium heat, bring to a simmer, cover and cook over a very low heat for 20–25 minutes until tender. Remove from the heat and leave to stand for 5 minutes, covered.

2. Put the beetroot, carrots, courgettes and walnuts into a large bowl. Add the millet, vinegar, oil, ½ teaspoon of salt and ¼ teaspoon of pepper and mix well. Add the egg and cornflour, mix again, then chill in the refrigerator for 2 hours.

3. Put the yogurt in a fine strainer over a bowl and drain for at least 30 minutes. Stir in the garlic and season to taste with salt and pepper.

4. Divide the beetroot mixture into five equal balls, then shape into five patties. Place a ridged griddle pan or large frying pan over a medium heat and coat with oil. Add the patties and cook for about 5 minutes on each side, turning carefully, until brown.

5. Spread the buns with the yogurt sauce and place the burgers in the buns, topped with the lettuce. Serve immediately.

JERUSALEM ARTICHOKES WITH TOMATO SAUCE

Not to be confused with the globe artichoke, this rather ugly-looking root vegetable is actually a member of the sunflower family. Although Jerusalem artichokes can be cooked in many ways, a simple, freshly made tomato sauce is the perfect way to show them off!

SERVES: 4   **PREP TIME: 10 MINS**   **COOK TIME: 30 MINS**

INGREDIENTS

450 g/1 lb Jerusalem artichokes, sliced

juice of ½ lemon

SAUCE

2 tbsp olive oil

1 large red onion, finely chopped

2 garlic cloves, finely chopped

500 g/1 lb 2 oz baby plum tomatoes, halved

3 sun-dried tomatoes, chopped, or 1 tbsp sun-dried tomato purée

200 ml/7 fl oz dry white wine

salt and pepper

2 tbsp chopped fresh basil leaves, to garnish

1. Put the artichokes into a bowl with the lemon juice, stir to coat, then set aside until ready to cook.

2. To make the sauce, heat the oil in a frying pan, add the onion and cook over a low heat, stirring occasionally, for 5 minutes. Add the garlic and cook for a further 2 minutes. Add the plum tomatoes, sun-dried tomatoes and wine. Season to taste, bring to the boil then reduce the heat and simmer, shaking the pan occasionally, for 10 minutes.

3. Meanwhile, bring a large saucepan of lightly salted water to the boil, add the artichokes and cook for 5–8 minutes, or until tender. Drain and transfer to a warmed serving dish. Top with the tomato mixture and garnish with basil. Serve immediately.

YAM-TOPPED COTTAGE PIE

SERVES: 4   **PREP TIME: 20 MINS**   **COOK TIME: 1½ HRS**

INGREDIENTS

2 tbsp vegetable oil
2 onions, chopped
115 g/4 oz carrots, finely chopped
115 g/4 oz swedes, finely chopped
450 g/1 lb fresh beef mince
1 tsp chopped fresh rosemary
1 tbsp chopped fresh parsley
1 tbsp tomato purée
1 tbsp plain flour
400 g/14 oz canned chopped tomatoes
300 ml/10 fl oz beef stock
½ tsp Worcestershire sauce
few drops hot pepper sauce

TOPPING

900 g/2 lb yams, cut into small even-sized pieces
55 g/2 oz butter
2 leeks, very thinly sliced
50 g/1¾ oz mature Cheddar cheese, grated
salt and pepper

1. Heat the oil in a large frying pan, add the onions, carrots and swedes and cook over a high heat for 5 minutes, stirring occasionally until the onions are beginning to brown. Using a slotted spoon, transfer the vegetables to a plate. Add the mince to the pan and brown over a high heat, stirring to break up.

2. Stir in the herbs, tomato purée and flour. Return the cooked vegetables to the pan with the tomatoes and stock. Add the Worcestershire sauce and the hot pepper sauce to taste. Bring to the boil, then reduce the heat and simmer for 30 minutes.

3. Meanwhile, to make the topping, bring a large saucepan of lightly salted water to the boil. Add the yams and cook for 15–20 minutes, or until tender. Drain and return to the pan with the butter and mash thoroughly. Season to taste with salt and pepper. Preheat the oven to 200°C/400°F/ Gas Mark 6.

4. Transfer the meat mixture to a baking dish, top with the mashed yams and spread evenly over the meat. Sprinkle the leeks over the top, then sprinkle over the cheese. Bake in the preheated oven for 35–40 minutes, or until golden. Serve immediately.

HOME FROM WORK & HUNGRY!

GET PREPPED!

Root vegetables can seem daunting to prepare so follow our simple guide to preparing beetroot and celeriac. It's easy when you know how!

1. To prepare a beetroot, remove the leaves and stalk with a knife. Leave approximately 2–3 cm/ 1 inch of the stalk intact.

2. Wash the beetroot thoroughly to clean off any dirt.

3. Wear rubber gloves when peeling the beetroot to avoid staining your hands.

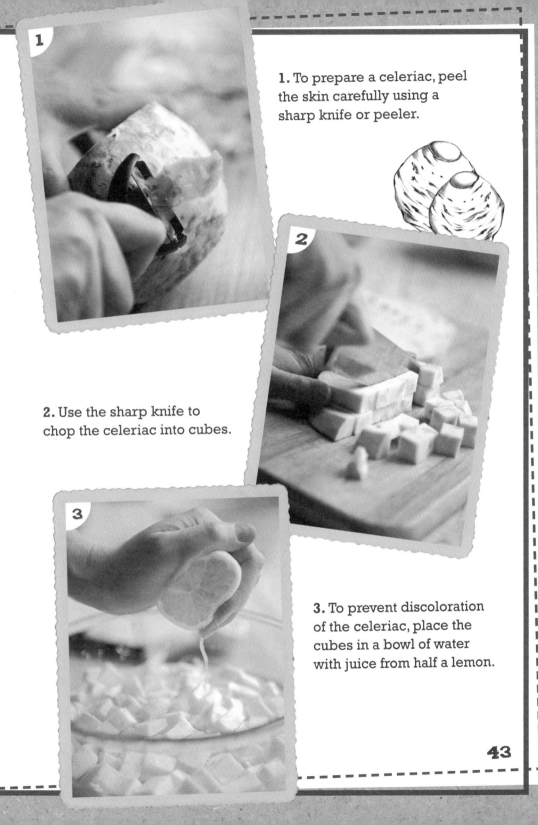

1. To prepare a celeriac, peel the skin carefully using a sharp knife or peeler.

2. Use the sharp knife to chop the celeriac into cubes.

3. To prevent discoloration of the celeriac, place the cubes in a bowl of water with juice from half a lemon.

CARROT & ORANGE STIR-FRY

This is a very quick and healthy dinner to get together after a busy day at work. The crisp vegetables combine deliciously with the sweet and sour sauce.

SERVES: 4   **PREP TIME: 10 MINS**   **COOK TIME: 10 MINS**

INGREDIENTS

2 tbsp sunflower oil
450 g/1 lb carrots, grated
225 g/8 oz leeks, shredded
2 oranges, peeled and segmented
2 tbsp tomato ketchup
1 tbsp demerara sugar
2 tbsp light soy sauce
100 g/3½ oz peanuts, chopped

1. Heat the oil in a large wok. Add the carrots and leeks to the wok and stir-fry for 2–3 minutes, or until the vegetables are just soft.

2. Add the oranges to the wok and heat through gently, ensuring that you do not break up the orange segments as you stir the mixture.

3. Mix the ketchup, sugar and soy sauce together in a small bowl.

4. Add the ketchup mixture to the wok and stir-fry for a further 2 minutes.

5. Transfer the stir-fry to warmed serving bowls and scatter over the peanuts. Serve immediately.

HERO TIPS

Carrots are one of healthiest roots and are rich in antioxidants which help to protect us from ill health. This stir-fry is extra healthy as the ingredients are cooked quickly, helping to preserve the vitamins in the vegetables.

NEW POTATO, FETA & HERB FRITTATA

SERVES: 4　　　　**PREP TIME: 10 MINS**　　　　**COOK TIME: 35 MINS**

INGREDIENTS

250 g/9 oz new potatoes, scrubbed

85 g/3 oz baby spinach leaves

5 eggs

1 tbsp chopped fresh dill, plus extra to garnish

1 tbsp snipped fresh chives, plus extra to garnish

115 g/4 oz feta cheese, crumbled

10 g/¼ oz butter

1 tbsp olive oil

salt and pepper

1. Bring a saucepan of lightly salted water to the boil, add the potatoes, bring back to the boil and cook for 25 minutes until tender. Place the spinach in a colander and drain the potatoes over the top to wilt the spinach. Set aside until cool enough to handle.

2. Cut the potatoes lengthways into 5-mm/¼-inch thick slices. Squeeze the excess water from the spinach leaves. Preheat the grill to high.

3. Lightly beat the eggs, dill and chives together. Season with pepper and add 85 g/3 oz of the cheese. Heat the butter and oil in a 20-cm/8-inch frying pan until melted and foaming. Add the potato slices and spinach and cook, stirring, for 1 minute. Pour the egg and cheese mixture over the top.

4. Cook, stirring, over a moderate heat for 1 minute until half set, then continue to cook for a further 2–3 minutes, without stirring, until set and golden brown underneath. Sprinkle the remaining cheese over the top, place under the preheated grill and cook for 2 minutes until golden brown on top. Serve hot or cold, sprinkled with chives and dill.

YAM, SWEDE & MUSHROOM HASH

A hearty hash that combines tastes and textures for a great breakfast or brunch dish. A few eggs broken into the mixture during the last few minutes of cooking makes a really tasty treat!

SERVES: 4   **PREP TIME: 15 MINS**   **COOK TIME: 30 MINS**

INGREDIENTS

3 tbsp olive oil
500 g/1 lb 2 oz yams, diced
280 g/10 oz swedes, diced
1 onion, chopped
175 g/6 oz streaky bacon, sliced, or lardons
250 g/9 oz mushrooms, sliced
4 eggs
salt and pepper
chopped fresh parsley, to garnish

1. Heat the oil in a large, lidded frying pan over a high heat. Add the yams and swedes, stir in the oil to coat and season to taste with salt and pepper. Cook, stirring occasionally for 10–15 minutes, or until the vegetables are just turning golden and soft.

2. Add the onion and bacon, stir well and continue to cook for 5 minutes until the onion is soft and the bacon is cooked. Stir in the mushrooms, cover the pan and cook for a further 5 minutes.

3. Make four indentations in the mixture and carefully break an egg into each one. Cover the pan and cook for a further 3–4 minutes, or until the egg whites are firm but the yolks are still soft. Garnish with parsley and serve immediately.

HERO TIPS

The yam is a very versatile vegetable – it can be roasted, fried, grilled, boiled and when grated, it can be used in desserts too!

JERUSALEM ARTICHOKE & HAZELNUT GRATIN

SERVES: 4   **PREP TIME: 15 MINS**   **COOK TIME: 45 MINS**

INGREDIENTS

750 g/1 lb 10 oz Jerusalem artichokes

squeeze of lemon juice

4 tbsp skinned hazelnuts, roughly chopped

40 g/1½ oz coarse ciabatta breadcrumbs

25 g/1 oz butter, plus extra for greasing

salt and pepper

steamed French beans, to serve

GARLIC CREAM

250 ml/9 fl oz whipping cream

7 large garlic cloves, lightly crushed

sliver of lemon peel

squeeze of lemon juice

1. To make the garlic cream, heat the cream, garlic and lemon peel in a saucepan over a medium heat, then simmer for about 5 minutes, until slightly reduced. Remove from the heat and leave to stand in a warm place.

2. Peel the artichokes, dropping them into water with a squeeze of lemon juice. Cut in half if they are large. Place in a steamer basket set over a saucepan of boiling water and steam for 8–10 minutes, until just tender at the edges. Leave to cool, then slice fairly thickly.

3. Strain the garlic cream into a jug. Add the lemon juice and season to taste.

4. Preheat the oven to 190°C/375°F/Gas Mark 5. Grease a 2-litre/3½-pint baking dish with butter. Arrange half the artichoke slices in the base of the prepared dish. Season with salt and pepper. Sprinkle with the nuts, then top with the remaining artichokes and a little more seasoning.

5. Pour over the warm garlic cream. Sprinkle with the breadcrumbs and dot with the butter.

6. Bake in the preheated oven for 30–35 minutes, until the artichokes are tender and the topping is golden and bubbling. Serve hot with steamed French beans.

3

4

6

CELERIAC SALAD WITH CRAB

SERVES: 4

PREP TIME: 15-20 MINS PLUS CHILLING

COOK TIME: 2 MINS

INGREDIENTS

450 g/1 lb celeriac, grated

juice of 1 lemon

250 g/9 oz fresh white crabmeat

chopped fresh dill or parsley, to garnish

mixed salad leaves, to serve

RÉMOULADE DRESSING

150 ml/5 fl oz mayonnaise

1 tbsp Dijon mustard

1½ tsp white wine vinegar

2 tbsp capers in brine, well rinsed

salt and white pepper

1. To make the dressing, put the mayonnaise in a bowl. Beat in the mustard, vinegar and capers with salt and white pepper to taste – the mixture should be piquant with a strong mustard flavour. Cover and chill until required.

2. Bring a large pan of salted water to a rolling boil. Add the grated celeriac and lemon juice to the water and blanch for 1½–2 minutes, or until it is just slightly tender. Rinse the celeriac well, then put it under cold running water to stop the cooking. Use your hands to squeeze out the excess moisture, then pat the celeriac dry with kitchen paper or a clean tea towel.

3. Stir the celeriac into the dressing, along with the crabmeat. Taste and adjust the seasoning, if necessary. Cover and chill for at least 30 minutes.

4. When ready to serve, spoon into bowls with the mixed salad leaves and garnish with dill or parsley.

HERO TIPS

Celeriac is a root vegetable variety of celery, which accounts for its similarity in flavour. It is also delicious when mashed, as an alternative to potato.

SPRING LAMB & TURNIP STEW

SERVES: 4-6   **PREP TIME: 15-20 MINS**   **COOK TIME: 1¼ HRS**

INGREDIENTS

40 g/1½ oz butter

2 tbsp sunflower oil, plus extra as needed

900 g/2 lb boned shoulder of lamb, trimmed and cut into large chunks, any bones reserved

2 shallots, finely chopped

1 tbsp sugar

1 litre/1¾ pints lamb stock

2 tbsp tomato purée

1 bouquet garni, with several parsley and thyme sprigs, 1 bay leaf and 1 small rosemary sprig

8 new potatoes, such as Charlotte, scrubbed and halved, if large

4 young turnips, quartered

12 baby carrots, scrubbed

140 g/5 oz frozen peas

salt and pepper

chopped fresh flat-leaf parsley, to garnish

baguette, to serve

1. Melt 30 g/1 oz of the butter with the oil in a large frying pan over a medium heat. Add the lamb, in batches to avoid overcrowding the pan, and fry, stirring, until coloured on all sides, adding extra oil, if necessary. Transfer the meat to a large casserole.

2. Melt the remaining butter with the fat left in the pan. Add the shallots and stir for 3 minutes, or until beginning to soften. Sprinkle with the sugar, increase the heat and continue stirring until the shallots caramelize, taking care that they do not burn. Transfer to the casserole and remove any charred bits from the base of the frying pan. Add half of the stock to the pan and bring to the boil, then tip this mixture into the casserole.

3. Add the remaining stock, tomato purée, bouquet garni and bones, if any, to the casserole. Season to taste with salt and pepper. Cover and bring to the boil. Reduce the heat and simmer for 45 minutes.

4. Add the potatoes, turnips and carrots and continue simmering for 15 minutes. Add the peas, then uncover and simmer for a further 5–10 minutes, or until the meat and all the vegetables are tender. Remove and discard the bones, if used, and the bouquet garni. Taste and adjust the seasoning, if necessary. Garnish with parsley and serve with a baguette.

RAW BEETROOT & PECAN SALAD

Originally grown just for its leaves, beetroot is also a rich source of folic acid and iron. Its strong, vibrant colour makes it a great addition to salads and soups as it adds real visual appeal to these dishes.

SERVES: 4 **PREP TIME: 10 MINS** **COOK TIME: NONE**

INGREDIENTS

175 g/6 oz fresh beetroot, roughly grated

8 radishes, thinly sliced

2 spring onions, finely chopped

25 g/1 oz pecan nuts, roughly chopped

8 red chicory leaves or Little Gem lettuce leaves

DRESSING

2 tbsp extra virgin olive oil

1 tbsp balsamic vinegar

2 tsp creamed horseradish sauce

salt and pepper

1. Combine the beetroot, radishes, spring onions and pecans in a bowl and toss well to mix evenly.

2. Place all the dressing ingredients in a small bowl and whisk lightly with a fork. Season to taste with salt and pepper and pour over the vegetables in the bowl, tossing to coat evenly.

3. Arrange the chicory or lettuce leaves on a serving platter and spoon the salad over them.

4. Serve the salad cold on its own or as an accompaniment to main dishes.

PARSNIP LAYERED CASSEROLE

SERVES: 4-6   **PREP TIME: 20 MINS**   **COOK TIME: 1 HR**

INGREDIENTS

3 tbsp olive oil

600 g/1 lb 5 oz parsnips, thinly sliced

1 tsp fresh thyme leaves

1 tsp caster sugar

300 ml/10 fl oz double cream

600 g/1 lb 5 oz tomatoes, thinly sliced

1 tsp dried oregano

150 g/5½ oz Cheddar cheese, grated

salt and pepper

1. Preheat the oven to 180°C/350°F/Gas Mark 4.

2. Heat the oil in a frying pan over a medium heat, add the parsnips, thyme, sugar and salt and pepper to taste and cook, stirring frequently, for 6–8 minutes until golden and softened.

3. Spread half the parsnips over the base of a gratin dish. Pour over half the cream, then arrange half the tomatoes in an even layer across the parsnips. Season to taste with salt and pepper and scatter over half the oregano. Sprinkle over half the Cheddar cheese. Top with the remaining parsnips and tomatoes. Sprinkle with the remaining oregano, season to taste with salt and pepper and pour over the remaining cream. Scatter over the remaining cheese.

4. Cover with foil and bake in the preheated oven for 40 minutes, or until the parsnips are tender. Remove the foil and return to the oven for a further 5–10 minutes until the top is golden and bubbling. Serve immediately.

POTATO & RADISH SALAD

This salad is based on a traditional Italian recipe, known as Country Salad, from the province of Trento. They also sometimes serve this with cubes of Italian cheese added, such as Grana Padano.

SERVES: 4

PREP TIME: 20 MINS PLUS RESTING

COOK TIME: 35 MINS

INGREDIENTS

300 g/10½ oz new potatoes

200 g/7 oz small cauliflower florets

4 tbsp extra virgin olive oil, plus extra if needed

4½ tsp red wine vinegar, plus extra if needed

200 g/7 oz fine French beans, cut into bite-sized pieces

4 spring onions, finely chopped

1 radish, thinly sliced

85 g/3 oz baby spinach leaves

2 tbsp toasted pine nuts

2 tbsp raisins or sultanas

salt and pepper

radicchio leaves and ciabatta bread, to serve

1. Bring two saucepans of lightly salted water to the boil. Add the potatoes to one pan, bring back to the boil and cook for 20–25 minutes, until tender. Add the cauliflower florets to the other pan, bring back to the boil and cook for 5 minutes, or until tender-crisp.

2. Meanwhile, whisk together the oil, vinegar, and salt and pepper to taste in a serving bowl.

3. Use a large slotted spoon to remove the cauliflower florets from the pan, shaking off the excess water, and stir them into the dressing in the bowl.

4. Drop the beans into the cauliflower cooking water, bring back to the boil and cook for 5 minutes, or until tender-crisp. Drain well, then stir into the serving bowl.

5. Drain the potatoes and cool slightly under cold running water. Peel and cut into bite-sized pieces, then stir into the dressing together with the spring

onions and radish. Make sure all the vegetables are coated with dressing, then set aside for at least 1 hour.

6. When ready to serve, line a platter with radicchio leaves. Stir the spinach into the serving bowl and add extra oil, vinegar and salt and pepper, if desired. Stir in the pine nuts and raisins.

7. Spoon the salad onto the radicchio leaves, adding any dressing left in the bowl. Serve with plenty of ciabatta bread to mop up the dressing.

POTATO, BROCCOLI & PEANUT BAKE

SERVES: 4   **PREP TIME: 15 MINS**   **COOK TIME: 50 MINS**

INGREDIENTS

450 g/1 lb new potatoes, sliced
1 tbsp olive oil
½ small onion, finely chopped
400 ml/14 fl oz coconut milk
8 tbsp crunchy peanut butter
1 tbsp soy sauce
2 tsp sugar
½ tsp dried red chilli flakes
200 g/7 oz broccoli florets
60 g/2¼ oz unsalted peanuts
2 tsp melted margarine
salt and pepper

1. Preheat the oven to 190°C/375°F/Gas Mark 5.

2. Bring a large saucepan of lightly salted water to the boil. Add the potatoes, bring back to the boil and cook for 8–10 minutes, or until slightly softened. Drain and set aside.

3. Heat the oil in a saucepan over a medium heat. Fry the onion for 2 minutes, then stir in the coconut milk, peanut butter, soy sauce, sugar and chilli flakes. Bring to the boil and stir well to ensure the ingredients are well combined. Reduce the heat and simmer for 5 minutes.

4. Meanwhile, place the broccoli in a steamer and lightly steam for 4–5 minutes, or until just tender.

5. Stir the broccoli and peanuts into the sauce, season to taste and transfer to a wide, square baking dish.

6. Cover the mixture with the cooked potato slices, dot with the melted margarine and season with pepper. Bake in the preheated oven for 20–25 minutes, or until the potatoes are golden. Leave to cool for 5 minutes before serving.

PAN-COOKED TUNA WITH RADISH RELISH

Borrowing from the Japanese tradition of pickling vegetables, the radishes and cucumber are marinated in a delicious mix of sweet and sour, which goes very well with the tuna.

SERVES: 4

PREP TIME: 15 MINS PLUS MARINATING

COOK TIME: 10 MINS

INGREDIENTS
4 x 150 g/5 oz tuna steaks
1 tbsp sesame seeds
cooked rice, to serve (optional)

MARINADE
2 tbsp dark soy sauce
2 tbsp sunflower oil
1 tbsp sesame oil
1 tbsp rice vinegar
1 tsp grated fresh ginger

RELISH
½ cucumber, peeled
1 bunch red radishes, trimmed

1. Place the tuna steaks in a dish and sprinkle over the sesame seeds, pressing them in with the back of a spoon so they stick to the fish.

2. To make the marinade, whisk together all the ingredients. Transfer 3 tablespoons of the marinade to a medium-sized bowl. Pour the remaining marinade over the fish, turning each steak to coat lightly. Cover and chill for 1 hour.

3. Slice the cucumber and radishes very thinly and add to the marinade in the bowl. Toss the vegetables to coat, then cover and chill.

4. Heat a large, heavy-based frying pan over a high heat. Add the steaks and cook for 3–4 minutes on each side depending on the thickness of the fish. Serve immediately with the radish relish and rice (if using).

HERO TIPS

Use a ridged frying pan to create attractive dark stripes on the tuna steaks or cook the steaks on a grill on a barbecue.

STIR-FRIED CHICKEN & SWEDE

SERVES: 4

PREP TIME: 15 MINS PLUS MARINATING

COOK TIME: 15-20 MINS

INGREDIENTS

4 skinless, boneless chicken breasts, about 115 g/4 oz each

3 tbsp vegetable oil

225 g/8 oz swedes, finely shredded

3 red, orange or yellow peppers, deseeded and cut into thin strips

4 fine dried egg noodle nests

chopped fresh coriander, to garnish

MARINADE

1 red chilli, deseeded and finely chopped

2.5-cm/1-inch piece fresh ginger, grated

2 garlic cloves, finely chopped

2 tbsp tomato ketchup

2 tbsp Chinese plum sauce

2 tbsp dark soy sauce

1. Cut the chicken breasts into 2.5-cm/1-inch pieces and place in a bowl. Add all the marinade ingredients and stir to coat the chicken. Cover and leave to stand at room temperature for 15 minutes, or chill in the refrigerator for up to 3 hours.

2. Heat 1 tablespoon of the oil in a wok or large frying pan, then add the swedes and peppers. Cook, stirring occasionally, for 8–10 minutes, or until the vegetables begin to soften. Using a slotted spoon, transfer to a warmed plate.

3. Heat the remaining oil in the wok and add the chicken and marinade. Cook, for 4–5 minutes, stirring, or until the chicken is cooked through and shows no traces of pink. Return the vegetables to the wok and continue to cook, stirring occasionally, until heated through.

4. Meanwhile, bring a small saucepan of water to the boil and add the noodles. Bring back to the boil, then simmer for 3 minutes, or until the noodles are cooked. Drain and divide between four serving plates. Top with the chicken and vegetables and garnish with coriander. Serve immediately.

LET ME ENTERTAIN YOU!

SWEET POTATO RAVIOLI WITH SAGE BUTTER

SERVES: 4

PREP TIME: 30 MINS PLUS CHILLING

COOK TIME: 30 MINS

INGREDIENTS

400 g/14 oz type 00 pasta flour

4 eggs, beaten

semolina, for dusting

salt

FILLING

500 g/1 lb 2 oz sweet potatoes

3 tbsp olive oil

1 large onion, finely chopped

1 garlic clove, crushed

1 tsp chopped fresh thyme

2 tbsp runny honey

salt and pepper

SAGE BUTTER

50 g/1¾ oz butter

1 bunch of fresh sage leaves, finely chopped, plus extra leaves to garnish

1. To make the pasta dough, sift the flour into a large bowl or food processor. Add the eggs and bring the mixture together or process to make a soft but not sticky dough. Turn out onto a work surface lightly dusted with semolina and knead for 4–5 minutes, until smooth. Cover with clingfilm and chill in the refrigerator for at least 30 minutes.

2. For the filling, peel the sweet potatoes and cut into chunks. Cook in a saucepan of boiling water for 20 minutes, or until tender. Drain and mash.

3. Heat the oil in a frying pan over a medium heat, add the onion and cook, stirring frequently, for 4–5 minutes, until softened but not coloured. Stir the onion into the mashed potatoes and add the garlic and thyme. Drizzle with the honey and season to taste with salt and pepper. Set aside.

4. Using a pasta machine, roll the pasta out to a thickness of about 1 mm/$\frac{1}{32}$ inch (or use a rolling pin on a work surface lightly dusted with semolina).

5. Cut the pasta in half. Place teaspoonfuls of the filling at evenly spaced intervals across half of the pasta. Brush around the filling with a small amount of water and cover with the second half of the pasta. Press lightly around the filling to seal and cut into

squares with a sharp knife or pastry wheel. Lay the ravioli out on a sheet of greaseproof paper that has been lightly dusted with semolina.

6. Bring a large saucepan of salted water to the boil and drop in the ravioli. Cook for 2–3 minutes, until the pasta rises to the surface and is tender but still firm to the bite.

7. Meanwhile, for the sage butter, melt the butter with the chopped sage in a small saucepan over a low heat.

8. Drain the ravioli and immediately toss with the sage butter. Serve immediately, garnished with sage leaves.

ROAST BEETROOT PARCELS

SERVES: 4

PREP TIME: 15 MINS PLUS COOLING

COOK TIME: 1½ HRS

INGREDIENTS

olive oil, for greasing and tossing

8 small beetroots, halved

4 fresh thyme sprigs

4 tbsp grated fresh horseradish, or grated horseradish from a jar

125 g/4½ oz unsalted butter

sea salt flakes and pepper

rocket leaves, to serve

POLENTA

850 ml/1½ pints water

175 g/6 oz quick-cook polenta

1 tsp salt

1. To make the polenta, bring the water to the boil in a large saucepan. Slowly add the polenta and salt, stirring constantly. Simmer, stirring frequently, for 5–10 minutes, until the mixture comes away from the side of the pan.

2. Grease a small roasting tin. Tip the polenta into the tin, level the surface and leave to cool.

3. Preheat the oven to 190°C/375°F/Gas Mark 5. Toss the beetroots with enough oil to coat.

4. Place 4 beetroot halves and a thyme sprig on a square of thick foil. Season to taste. Wrap in a loose parcel, sealing the edges. Repeat with the remaining beetroots and place on a baking sheet.

5. Roast in the preheated oven for about 1 hour or until just tender.

6. Meanwhile, mash the horseradish with the butter, ½ teaspoon of salt and ¼ teaspoon of pepper. Roll into a log using a piece of clingfilm and chill in the refrigerator.

7. Preheat the grill to high. Slice the polenta into four neat rectangles. Spread out in a grill pan, brush with oil and cook under a hot grill for 5 minutes. Turn and grill for a further 3 minutes, until crisp.

8. Arrange the polenta on serving plates. Place the beetroot and a slice of horseradish butter on top. Add a handful of rocket to each plate and serve immediately.

PUTTING DOWN ROOTS!

Even if you have only limited experience and limited space, there's no reason why you can't grow root vegetables. If you have just a balcony or patio, grow them in deep compost-filled containers such as tall terracotta pots or builders' buckets. There are also special planting bags for growing root vegetables in tight spaces. Ideally choose a space that gets sun for most of the day.

WHAT TO GROW

Roots that take forever to mature – swedes and parsnips, for example – are not the best choice. If you are time-poor, don't get carried away with attention-seeking varieties such as celeriac and salsify. Think about what you like to eat. Radishes may be easy to grow but pointless if they're a pet hate. Ultimately, it makes sense to stick to quick-growing varieties that are hard to find in the shops and have a high yield-to-space ratio.

Beetroot is a good no-nonsense choice for a beginner and has the advantage that you can also eat the leaves. The roots are fast growing, can be eaten at any size, and come in dazzling colours. Impress your guests with golden or pink-and-white candy-striped varieties. Sow in early spring for a mid-summer harvest, and continue sowing monthly

until mid-summer. The beetroot seed is actually a fruit containing two or three seeds. Several seedlings may emerge from each fruit, forming little clusters that need thinning. Use the smallest in salads and leave the strongest to grow on. They will be ready in 9–12 weeks. The last roots of the season will tough it out below ground if covered with straw or fleece, or they can be lifted and stored in a frost-free place.

Carrots are another rewarding crop, and one of the tastiest. There is a great choice of shapes, sizes and colours: blunt or wedge-shaped, dumpy or long, and if you don't like orange, go for white, purple or yellow. There are plenty to choose from in the catalogues. Carrots are fusspots about soil. Long varieties may become stunted in shallow soil, but short round varieties do well. Containers are a good solution if your soil isn't up to scratch. Sow them in late winter for a late-spring harvest. You can start pulling them once they are big enough to eat.

CARAMELIZED SWEDE, ONION & HAM PIE

SERVES: 4   **PREP TIME: 10 MINS**   **COOK TIME: 1 HR**

INGREDIENTS

600 g/1 lb 5 oz cooked ham, cubed
85 g/3 oz butter
2 onions, chopped
450 g/1 lb swede, cubed
1 tsp chopped fresh sage
25 g/1 oz plain flour, plus extra for dusting
600 ml/1 pint milk
325 g/11½ oz ready-made puff pastry, thawed if frozen
beaten egg, to glaze
salt and pepper

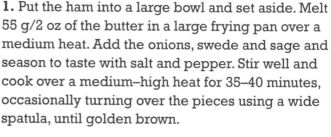

1. Put the ham into a large bowl and set aside. Melt 55 g/2 oz of the butter in a large frying pan over a medium heat. Add the onions, swede and sage and season to taste with salt and pepper. Stir well and cook over a medium–high heat for 35–40 minutes, occasionally turning over the pieces using a wide spatula, until golden brown.

2. Meanwhile, melt the remaining butter in a small saucepan over a medium heat. Add the flour and cook, stirring, for 1–2 minutes. Gradually add the milk, stirring to make a smooth sauce. Remove from the heat and season to taste with salt and pepper.

3. Preheat the oven to 220°C/425°F/Gas Mark 7. Roll out the pastry on a lightly floured surface to a rectangle slightly larger than the top of a 26 x 18-cm/10½ x 7-inch pie dish.

4. When the vegetables are caramelized, add to the bowl with the ham, then add the white sauce, stirring gently to combine. Transfer the mixture to a pie dish, brush the rim with the beaten egg and then lay the pastry over the filling. Press the pastry to the rim, then trim off the excess and cut out shapes to decorate the top, if liked. Brush the pastry with the beaten egg and cook in the oven for 15–20 minutes, or until the pastry is puffed and golden. Serve immediately.

POTATO GNOCCHI WITH WALNUT PESTO

SERVES: 4   **PREP TIME: 30 MINS**   **COOK TIME: 45 MINS**

INGREDIENTS

450 g/1 lb floury potatoes, washed but not peeled

55 g/2 oz freshly grated Parmesan cheese

1 egg, beaten

200 g/7 oz plain flour, plus extra for dusting

salt and pepper

WALNUT PESTO

40 g/1½ oz fresh flat-leaf parsley, chopped

2 tbsp capers, rinsed and chopped

2 garlic cloves, chopped

175 ml/6 fl oz extra virgin olive oil

70 g/2½ oz walnut pieces

40 g/1½ oz freshly grated Parmesan cheese

salt and pepper

1. Bring a large saucepan of lightly salted water to the boil. Add the potatoes, bring back to the boil and cook for 30–35 minutes, until tender. Drain well and leave to cool slightly.

2. Meanwhile, to make the pesto, put the parsley, capers and garlic into a mortar with the oil, walnuts, and salt and pepper to taste. Pound to a coarse paste using a pestle. Add the cheese and stir well.

3. When the potatoes are just cool enough to handle, peel off the skins and pass the flesh through a sieve into a large bowl or press through a potato ricer. While still hot, season well with salt and pepper and add the cheese.

4. Beat in the egg and sift in the flour. Lightly mix together, then turn out onto a lightly floured work surface. Lightly knead until the mixture becomes a smooth dough. If it is too sticky, add a little more flour.

5. Using your hands, roll out the dough on a lightly floured work surface into a long log.

6. Cut the log into 2.5-cm/1-inch pieces and gently press each piece with a fork to give the traditional ridged effect of gnocchi. Transfer the pieces to a floured baking sheet and cover with a clean tea towel.

7. Bring a large saucepan of water to the boil, add the gnocchi, in small batches, and cook for 1–2 minutes.

8. Remove with a slotted spoon and transfer to a warmed dish to keep warm while you cook the remaining gnocchi. Serve the gnocchi on warmed plates, topped with a good spoonful of the pesto.

CARROT TARTE TATIN

SERVES: 4　　　**PREP TIME: 15 MINS**　　　**COOK TIME: 45 MINS**

INGREDIENTS

600 g/1 lb 5 oz young carrots, cut into 2.5-cm/1-inch chunks

2 tbsp clear honey

25 g/1 oz butter

1 small bunch fresh thyme, chopped

350 g/12 oz ready-made puff pastry, thawed if frozen

plain flour, for dusting

salt and pepper

1. Bring a large saucepan of lightly salted water to the boil. Add the carrots, bring back to the boil and cook for 10–15 minutes, until just tender. Drain, toss with the honey, butter and thyme and season to taste with salt and pepper.

2. Preheat the oven to 200°C/400°F/Gas Mark 6. Spoon the carrots over the base of a 20-cm/8-inch tarte tatin tin or round cake tin with a depth of about 3 cm/1¼ inches. Roast in the preheated oven for 15 minutes, or until the carrots are caramelized. Remove the tin from the oven but leave the oven on.

3. Roll out the pastry on a floured work surface into a round large enough to fit the tin and give a 2-cm/¾-inch overlap. Lay the pastry carefully over the carrots and tuck the edges down between the carrots and the side of the tin to make a border. Bake in the oven for 15 minutes, or until the pastry is puffed and golden.

4. Remove the tart from the oven and turn the tin over onto a plate to release.

5. Cut the tart into slices and serve immediately.

SPICED PARSNIP GRATIN WITH GINGER CREAM

This is a deceptively easy recipe to make, but it looks and tastes really impressive so is ideal for dinner parties! Most of the work is done in the oven, leaving you free to prepare the rest of the meal.

SERVES: 4   **PREP TIME: 15 MINS**   **COOK TIME: 40 MINS**

INGREDIENTS

butter, for greasing

3 large parsnips, about 750 g/1 lb 10 oz, thinly sliced

425 ml/15 fl oz double cream

250 ml/9 fl oz vegetable stock

1 garlic clove, crushed

2.5-cm/1-inch piece fresh ginger, roughly chopped and crushed in a garlic press

¼ tsp freshly ground white pepper

⅛ tsp freshly grated nutmeg, plus extra to garnish

sea salt

snipped chives, to garnish

1. Lightly grease a large gratin dish. Place the parsnips in a steamer basket set over a saucepan of boiling water. Steam for 3 minutes, until barely tender, shaking halfway through cooking. Tip into the prepared dish and lightly season with salt.

2. Preheat the oven to 180°C/350°F/Gas Mark 4. Gently heat the cream and stock in a saucepan with the garlic and ginger. Do not allow the mixture to boil. Add the pepper, nutmeg and sea salt to taste.

3. Pour the hot cream mixture over the parsnips. Cover the dish with foil and bake in the preheated oven for 20 minutes, with an oven tray underneath to catch any drips.

4. Remove the foil and bake for a further 15–20 minutes, until golden on top.

5. Sprinkle with a little more nutmeg and some chives and serve immediately.

BEETROOT, LOBSTER & SPINACH RISOTTO

SERVES: 4   **PREP TIME: 15 MINS**   **COOK TIME: 30 MINS**

INGREDIENTS

1.5 litres/2¾ pints vegetable
stock or chicken stock

25 g/1 oz butter

2 tbsp olive oil

1 small onion, diced

280 g/10 oz risotto rice

100 ml/3½ fl oz dry white wine

5 small raw beetroots, grated

1 tsp grated horseradish

juice of ½ lemon

175 g/6 oz baby leaf spinach

225 g/8 oz ready-to-eat lobster
meat or crabmeat

115 g/4 oz freshly grated
Parmesan cheese

salt and pepper

crème fraîche, to serve

1. Bring the stock to the boil in a large saucepan, then simmer over a low heat. Meanwhile, heat the butter and oil in a separate large saucepan over a medium heat, add the onion and fry for 3 minutes. Add the rice and stir to coat with the butter and oil. Cook for a further 2 minutes. Add the wine and simmer for 2 minutes, or until absorbed.

2. Add the beetroots and stir well. Add 2 ladles of hot stock to the pan, then cover and cook for 2 minutes, or until absorbed. Stir well and add another ladle of stock. Stir constantly until the stock is absorbed, then add another ladle. Continue adding the stock, one ladle at a time, until it has all been absorbed and the rice is almost cooked.

3. Stir in the horseradish and lemon juice, then add the spinach and season to taste with salt and pepper. Divide between warmed bowls, top with the lobster meat and cheese and serve immediately, accompanied by the crème fraîche.

BAKED ROOT VEGETABLE & ROSEMARY CAKE

This is an unusual way to serve a varied selection of root vegetables and it is subtly flavoured with rosemary and lemon to make something really special.

SERVES: 4   **PREP TIME: 15-20 MINS**   **COOK TIME: 1 HR**

INGREDIENTS

olive oil, for greasing
300 g/10½ oz parsnips, roughly grated
300 g/10½ oz carrots, roughly grated
300 g/10½ oz celeriac, roughly grated
1 onion, roughly grated
2 tbsp chopped fresh rosemary
3 tbsp lemon juice
salt and pepper
rosemary sprigs, to garnish

1. Preheat the oven to 190°C/375°F/Gas Mark 5. Grease a 20-cm/8-inch round cake tin and line with baking paper.

2. Place the parsnip, carrot and celeriac in separate, small bowls.

3. Mix together the onion, rosemary and lemon juice in a small bowl. Add a third of the onion mixture to each vegetable bowl, season to taste with salt and pepper, and stir to mix evenly.

4. Spoon the parsnips into the prepared tin, spreading evenly and pressing down lightly. Top with the carrots, press lightly, then add the celeriac.

5. Top the cake with a piece of lightly oiled kitchen foil and press down to flatten the contents. Tuck the foil over the edges of the tin to seal. Place on a baking sheet and bake in the preheated oven for about 1 hour, or until tender.

6. Remove the foil and turn out the cake onto a warmed plate. Leave to cool for 5 minutes and then slice and serve, garnished with rosemary sprigs.

SLOW-COOKED POTATO STEW

SERVES: 4   **PREP TIME: 20 MINS**   **COOK TIME: 1 HR**

INGREDIENTS

700 g/1 lb 9 oz waxy potatoes,
cut into 2.5-cm/1-inch cubes

25 g/1 oz butter

2 tbsp olive oil

55 g/2 oz pancetta or bacon,
diced

1 onion, finely chopped

1 garlic clove, finely chopped

1 celery stick, finely chopped

400 g/14 oz canned chopped
tomatoes

2 tbsp tomato purée

brown sugar, to taste

1 tbsp chopped fresh marjoram

100 ml/3½ fl oz vegetable stock

salt and pepper

1. Parboil the potatoes in a saucepan of lightly salted boiling water for 5 minutes. Drain and set aside.

2. Melt the butter with the oil in a saucepan. Add the pancetta, onion, garlic and celery and cook over a low heat, stirring occasionally, for 5 minutes, until softened. Stir in the tomatoes, tomato purée, sugar to taste, marjoram and stock and season to taste with salt and pepper. Increase the heat to medium and bring to the boil. Gently stir in the potatoes, reduce the heat to very low, cover and simmer, stirring occasionally, for 45–50 minutes, until the potatoes are tender and the sauce has thickened. (Use a fork to stir gently to avoid breaking up the potatoes.)

3. Taste and adjust the seasoning, adding salt and pepper if needed. Transfer the mixture to warmed bowls and serve immediately.

PORK BRAISED WITH CELERIAC & ORANGE

In many parts of China, slow-cooked casseroles are popular during the cold winter months. Orange, star anise and chilli bean sauce are particularly good with pork and celeriac.

SERVES: 4

PREP TIME: 20 MINS PLUS MARINATING

COOK TIME: 2¼ HRS

INGREDIENTS

900 g/2 lb pork shoulder, cubed

3 tbsp olive oil

500 g/1 lb 2 oz celeriac, cut into 5-cm/2-inch sticks

2 small leeks, cut into 5-cm/2-inch strips

3 carrots, cut into 5-cm/2-inch strips

200 ml/7 fl oz chicken stock

cooked rice, to serve

MARINADE

thinly pared rind and juice of 1 orange

1–2 whole star anise

2 tbsp dark soy sauce

1 tbsp honey

2.5 cm/1-inch piece fresh ginger, grated

3 garlic cloves, finely chopped

2 tsp Chinese chilli bean sauce

1. Place the pork in a large bowl. Add all the marinade ingredients, stir well, cover and chill in the refrigerator for 3 hours or overnight.

2. Preheat the oven to 120°C/250°F/Gas Mark ½. Remove the pork from the marinade using a slotted spoon and transfer to a plate, discarding the orange peel and star anise. Reserve the marinade.

3. Heat 1 tablespoon of the oil in a large frying pan and add half the pork pieces. Cook for 2 minutes, then turn the pieces over and cook for a further 2 minutes.

4. Transfer the pork and the cooking juices to a casserole dish. Repeat with 1 tablespoon of the oil and the remaining pork and transfer to the casserole dish.

5. Add the remaining oil to the pan, then add the celeriac, leeks and carrots and cook, stirring occasionally, until the leeks are soft.

6. Transfer the vegetables to the casserole dish, strain the marinade over the vegetables and add

the stock. Cover and cook in the preheated oven for 1 hour.

7. Stir the pork and vegetables, cover and return to the oven for a further 1 hour. Serve with cooked rice.

WHAT'S COOKING?

Cooking root vegetables in different ways produces different tastes and textures. Regardless of how you decide to cook them, use roots of a similar size, or cut them into even-sized pieces so that they cook at the same rate. Peeled potato, celeriac and parsnip should be put straight into water to stop browning.

STEAMING

This is a healthy alternative to boiling, and a handy technique for partially softening root vegetables before roasting or grilling. Since they aren't in direct contact with the liquid, they don't become waterlogged and fewer nutrients leach into the water. If you have never tried steaming, it's worth investing in a 'universal' steamer insert.

BOILING

Boiling is the simplest method for the majority of roots, but remember that the turbulent action of fast-boiling liquid can break up the starchier ones – Jerusalem artichokes, yams and floury potatoes, for example. It's best to start them off in cold water and turn down the heat once boiling, so they cook at a gentler pace.

STOVE-TOP GRILLING

This works well for denser roots, such as swede or celeriac. Lightly steam them, then cut into thick slices and brush with oil. You will need a heavy-based cast-iron pan, preferably with ridges for producing appetizing brown stripes. The direct heat quickly seals in the juices and crisps the outside.

FRYING

Frying brings anaemic-looking roots to life. They develop intense flavours, a crisp texture and become sweetly caramelized. Slice them first and fry in a roomy pan. If you overcrowd them, they will steam rather than browning and crisping.

ROASTING

The dry heat of the oven caramelizes natural sugars in root vegetables, making them brown and sticky in the process. Give them plenty of space and use a shallow roasting tray rather than a high-sided one, so that heat can circulate unimpeded.

CREAMED CHICKEN WITH JERUSALEM ARTICHOKES

SERVES: 2　　　　**PREP TIME: 15 MINS**　　　　**COOK TIME: 25 MINS**

INGREDIENTS

25 g/1 oz butter

1 onion, finely chopped

200 g/7 oz Jerusalem artichokes, sliced

200 ml/7 fl oz water

100 ml/3½ fl oz white wine

2 fresh tarragon sprigs or ½ tsp dried tarragon

2 skinless, boneless chicken breasts, about 115 g/4 oz each

1 tsp Dijon mustard

3 tbsp crème fraîche

salt and pepper

chopped fresh tarragon, to garnish (optional)

cooked rice, to serve

1. Melt the butter in a large frying pan over a medium heat, add the onions and cook for 4–5 minutes, or until soft. Add the artichokes, water, wine and tarragon. Bring to the boil, then reduce the heat and simmer, covered, for 5 minutes, or until the artichokes are just tender.

2. Cut each chicken breast into 4 pieces and add to the pan. Season with salt and pepper and continue to cook, stirring, for 10 minutes, or until the chicken is cooked through and shows no traces of pink.

3. Remove the tarragon sprigs and stir in the mustard and crème fraîche. Increase the heat and leave the sauce to bubble and thicken. Divide between two warmed plates and garnish with chopped tarragon, if using. Serve immediately with cooked rice.

SWEET POTATO CURRY WITH LENTILS

This sweet potato curry is very nutritious and filling, so ideal for spice lovers with big appetites! Sweet potato is high in carotenes, lowers cholesterol, and is a good food to help dieters ward off hunger.

SERVES: 4   **PREP TIME: 15 MINS**   **COOK TIME: 45 MINS**

INGREDIENTS

1 tsp vegetable oil

100 g/3½ oz sweet potato, cut into bite-sized cubes

75 g/2¾ oz potato, cut into bite-sized cubes

1 small onion, finely chopped

1 small garlic clove, finely chopped

1 small fresh green chilli, deseeded and chopped

½ tsp ground ginger

50 g/1¾ oz green lentils

75–100 ml/2½–3½ fl oz hot vegetable stock

½ tsp garam masala

1 tbsp natural yogurt

pepper

1. Heat the oil in a saucepan with a lid and sauté the sweet potato over a medium heat, turning occasionally, for 5 minutes.

2. Meanwhile, cook the potato in a saucepan of boiling water for 6 minutes, until almost cooked. Drain and set aside.

3. Remove the sweet potato from the pan with a slotted spoon, then add the onion to the pan. Cook, stirring occasionally, for 5 minutes, or until transparent. Add the garlic, chilli and ginger and stir for 1 minute.

4. Return the sweet potato to the pan with the boiled potato and the lentils, half the stock, the garam masala and pepper to taste. Stir well to combine, bring to a simmer and cover.

5. Reduce the heat and simmer for 20 minutes, adding the rest of the stock if the curry looks too dry. Stir in the yogurt and serve immediately.

A BIT ON THE SIDE!

ROASTED ROOT VEGETABLES

SERVES: 4-6 **PREP TIME: 15 MINS** **COOK TIME: 1 HR**

INGREDIENTS

3 parsnips, cut into
5-cm/2-inch chunks

4 baby turnips, cut into quarters

3 carrots, cut into
5-cm/2-inch chunks

450 g/1 lb butternut
squash, cut into 5-cm/
2-inch chunks

450 g/1 lb sweet potatoes,
cut into 5-cm/2-inch chunks

2 garlic cloves, finely chopped

2 tbsp chopped fresh rosemary

2 tbsp chopped fresh thyme

2 tsp chopped fresh sage

3 tbsp olive oil

salt and pepper

2 tbsp chopped fresh mixed
herbs, such as parsley, thyme
and mint, to garnish

1. Preheat the oven to 220°C/425°F/Gas Mark 7.

2. Arrange all the vegetables in a single layer in a large roasting tin. Scatter over the garlic, rosemary, thyme and sage. Pour over the oil and season well with salt and pepper.

3. Toss all the ingredients together until they are well mixed and coated with the oil (you can leave them to marinate at this stage to allow the flavours to be absorbed).

4. Roast the vegetables at the top of the preheated oven for 50–60 minutes, until they are cooked and nicely browned. Turn the vegetables over halfway through the cooking time. Serve immediately, garnished with the mixed herbs.

HERO TIPS

These delicious roasted root vegetables are crisp and golden on the outside and soft and fluffy on the inside! They make a great accompaniment to a traditional roast dinner or to any baked dish, such as a lasagne or a tuna casserole.

COLCANNON MASH WITH LEEK & CABBAGE

This fluffy mash with leeks and cabbage is a classic Irish vegetable dish that is often served on St Patrick's Day. The dish even has a traditional Irish folk song written about it, of the same name!

SERVES: 4　　　　**PREP TIME: 15 MINS**　　　　**COOK TIME: 20-25 MINS**

INGREDIENTS

225 g/8 oz green cabbage, shredded

225 g/8 oz floury potatoes, such as King Edward, Maris Piper or Desirée, diced

1 large leek, chopped

3 tbsp milk

pinch of freshly grated nutmeg

knob of butter

salt and pepper

1. Cook the shredded cabbage in a saucepan of boiling salted water for 7–10 minutes. Drain thoroughly and set aside.

2. Meanwhile, bring a separate saucepan of salted water to the boil and add the potatoes and leek. Reduce the heat and simmer for 15–20 minutes, or until they are cooked through. Drain and then stir in the milk and the freshly grated nutmeg. Thoroughly mash the potatoes and leek together.

3. Add the drained cabbage to the mashed potato and leek mixture, season to taste and mix together well.

4. Spoon the mixture into a warmed serving dish, making a hollow in the centre with the back of a spoon. Place the butter in the hollow and serve the colcannon immediately, while it is still hot.

CRISPY POTATO SLICES

SERVES: 4 **PREP TIME: 10 MINS** **COOK TIME: 25 MINS**

INGREDIENTS

500 g/1 lb 2 oz firm-textured potatoes, such as Charlotte

55 g/2 oz goose or duck fat, or 40 g/1½ oz butter with 1 tbsp olive oil

salt

1. Bring a large saucepan of lightly salted water to the boil. Add the potatoes, bring back to the boil and cook for 5 minutes. Drain the potatoes and, when they are cool enough to handle, peel and cut into thin slices or small cubes.

2. Melt the fat or butter and oil in a large, heavy-based sauté pan or frying pan over a high heat, until hot but not smoking. Pour off any excess fat so you are left with 5 mm/¼ inch of fat.

3. Add the potatoes to the pan, spread out so they are evenly distributed, and reduce the heat to medium. Fry the potatoes, shaking the pan and turning them occasionally, for 10–12 minutes, or until they are golden brown and crisp on the outside. Use a slotted spoon to transfer the potatoes to a plate lined with kitchen paper and drain well. Season with salt and serve immediately.

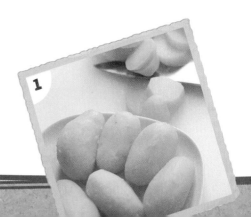

NEEPS & TATTIES MASH

This dish is a rustic Scottish mix of mashed swede (neeps) and potatoes (tatties), traditionally served on Burns Night with haggis. This dish also makes a good accompaniment to roast meats, sausages, stews or casseroles.

SERVES: 5   **PREP TIME: 15 MINS**   **COOK TIME: 20-25 MINS**

INGREDIENTS

450 g/1 lb swedes, diced

250 g/9 oz floury potatoes, such as King Edward, Maris Piper or Desirée, diced

55 g/2 oz butter, plus extra to serve

whole nutmeg, for grating

salt and pepper

fresh parsley sprigs, to garnish

1. Bring a large saucepan of lightly salted water to the boil. Add the swedes and potatoes and cook for 20 minutes until soft. Test with the point of a knife – if not cooked, return to the heat for a further 5 minutes. Drain well.

2. Return the swede and potatoes to the empty saucepan and heat for a few moments to ensure they are dry. Add the butter and mash with a potato masher until smooth.

3. Season well with salt and pepper and stir through. Grate nutmeg into the mash to taste and serve immediately, garnished with the parsley and with a knob of butter on top.

HERO TIPS

The swede is a cross between a cabbage and a turnip and is so named because it originally comes from Sweden. Another way to serve this dish is to add chives and onions to the recipe here – this version of the dish is known in Scotland as clapshot.

SUGAR-GLAZED PARSNIPS

These gently caramelized parsnips are a great dish to serve with roasted meats or a nut roast. They are also perfect for special occasions, such as Christmas or Easter dinners.

SERVES: 8　　　**PREP TIME: 5 MINS**　　　**COOK TIME: 40 MINS**

INGREDIENTS

24 small parsnips, sliced lengthways
about 1 tsp salt
115 g/4 oz butter
115 g/4 oz soft brown sugar

1. Place the parsnips in a saucepan, add just enough water to cover, then add the salt. Bring to the boil, reduce the heat, cover and simmer for 20–25 minutes, until tender. Drain well.

2. Melt the butter in a heavy-based pan or wok. Add the parsnips and toss well. Sprinkle with the sugar, then cook, stirring constantly to prevent the sugar from sticking to the pan or burning.

3. Cook the parsnips for 10–15 minutes, until golden and glazed. Transfer to a warmed serving dish and serve immediately.

HERO TIPS

The parsnip is a close relative of the carrot and is similarly good for your health. It contains lots of dietary fibre to aid the digestive system.

CARAMELIZED SWEET POTATOES

SERVES: 4　　　　**PREP TIME: 10 MINS**　　　**COOK TIME: 1¼ HRS**

INGREDIENTS

450 g/1 lb sweet potatoes, washed but not peeled

55 g/2 oz butter, plus extra for greasing

55 g/2 oz brown sugar, maple syrup or honey

2 tbsp orange or pineapple juice

55 g/2 oz pineapple pieces (optional)

pinch of ground cinnamon, nutmeg or mixed spice (optional)

salt

1. Bring a large saucepan of lightly salted water to the boil. Add the sweet potatoes, bring back to the boil and cook for about 30–45 minutes, until just tender. Remove from the heat and drain well. Leave to cool slightly, then peel.

2. Preheat the oven to 200°C/400°F/Gas Mark 6. Grease an ovenproof dish. Thickly slice the sweet potatoes and arrange in a single overlapping layer in the prepared dish.

3. Cut the butter into small cubes and dot over the top.

4. Sprinkle with the sugar and orange juice. Add the pineapple pieces, and spices, if using. Bake in the preheated oven for 30–40 minutes, basting occasionally, until golden brown.

5. Remove from the oven and serve hot, straight from the dish.

HERO TIPS

Sweet potatoes are low in calories and low on the glycaemic index and so are ideal foods for slimmers.

KEEP IT FRESH!

Root vegetables stay freshest in a cool, dark, dry, well-ventilated place, not necessarily in the refrigerator (see below). Freshly harvested, they can be stored for months in a cellar or frost-free shed. Depending on when they are harvested, shop-bought roots can be kept for several days in a cool room. Failing this, store them in a ventilated drawer (wicker or perforated metal), away from heat-producing appliances such as the stove or refrigerator, and preferably decanted into a light-excluding drawstring cotton bag to prevent sprouting. There are several on the market specifically for storing root vegetables.

Roots that can survive the chill of the refrigerator should be stored, unwashed, in the salad drawer where the temperature is less arctic. They are best wrapped in newspaper or a paper bag. Paper absorbs moisture, providing the slightly humid but well-ventilated atmosphere that most roots need. In some cases, a sealed plastic bag is preferable; radishes, for example, need an enclosed moist environment.

If you buy roots with leaves and stems, remove these before storing, leaving a short length of stem attached so as not to expose the flesh. Leaves may give the impression of freshness, but they rot quickly and the root itself loses moisture through them.

STORAGE TIMES

The following times are a guide for storing shop-bought vegetables in the refrigerator, a cool, dry place, or ventilated drawer. The time will depend on when they were harvested, where and how they have been stored after harvesting, and how long they have been on sale.

Beetroots: 7–10 days.

Carrots: young 3–4 days, mature 1–2 weeks.

Celeriacs: 1 week, wrapped in clingfilm to prevent drying.

Jerusalem artichokes: 7–10 days.

Parsnips: 1 week.

Potatoes: 1 week, ideally in a light-proof cloth bag. Do not store in the refrigerator as they will become unpleasantly sweet.

Radishes: 3–4 days in the refrigerator, wrapped in damp paper towels in a sealed plastic bag.

Swedes: 3–4 weeks.

Sweet potatoes: 3–4 weeks.

Turnips: young 1 week, mature 2–3 weeks.

Yams: 7–10 days. Do not store in the refrigerator as this causes rotting.

ROOT VEGETABLE FRIES

These root vegetable fries make a great alternative to traditional potato chips or wedges. They use less oil than traditional fries as well and so are better for you too!

SERVES: 4   **PREP TIME: 10 MINS**   **COOK TIME: 25 MINS**

INGREDIENTS

900 g/2 lb any combination of parsnips, swedes, turnips and carrots, cut into 5-mm/ ¼-inch strips

2 tbsp vegetable oil

1 tsp salt

sea salt

1. Preheat the oven to 230°C/450°F/Gas Mark 8.

2. Toss the cut vegetables with the oil and salt. Spread the vegetables in a single layer on a large baking sheet and bake in the preheated oven for about 20 minutes, flipping them halfway through cooking, until they are golden brown and cooked through. Remove from the oven and preheat the grill to medium.

3. Place under the preheated grill for 2–3 minutes, until they begin to crisp up. Flip them over and return them to the grill for a further 2 minutes to crisp the other side. Serve immediately, sprinkled with sea salt.

ROASTED POTATO WEDGES WITH SHALLOTS

SERVES: 4   **PREP TIME: 10 MINS**   **COOK TIME: 1 HR**

INGREDIENTS

1 kg/2 lb 4 oz small potatoes
6 tbsp olive oil
2 fresh rosemary sprigs
150 g/5½ oz baby shallots
2 garlic cloves, sliced
salt and pepper

1. Preheat the oven to 200°C/400°F/Gas Mark 6. Peel and cut each potato into wedges. Put the potatoes in a large saucepan of lightly salted water and bring to the boil. Reduce the heat and simmer for 5 minutes.

2. Heat the oil in a large roasting tin on the hob. Drain the potatoes well and add to the roasting tin. Strip the leaves from the rosemary sprigs, chop finely and sprinkle over the potatoes.

3. Roast the potatoes in the preheated oven for 35 minutes, turning twice during cooking. Add the shallots and garlic and roast for a further 15 minutes, until golden brown. Season to taste with salt and pepper.

4. Transfer to a warmed serving dish and serve immediately.

HERO TIPS

It is best to use a small, firm variety of potato for this recipe, such as Charlotte potatoes. Potatoes are rich in minerals that help the functioning of your brain and muscles, to keep you thinking and moving youthfully!

SWEET POTATO MASH WITH PARSLEY BUTTER

SERVES: 4　　　　**PREP TIME: 10 MINS**　　　　**COOK TIME: 25 MINS**

INGREDIENTS

70 g/2½ oz butter, softened

2 tbsp chopped fresh parsley

900 g/2 lb sweet potatoes, scrubbed

salt

1. Reserving 25 g/1 oz, put the butter into a bowl with the parsley and beat together. Turn out onto a square of foil or clingfilm, shape into a block and chill in the refrigerator until required.

2. Cut the sweet potatoes into even-sized chunks. Bring a large saucepan of lightly salted water to the boil, add the sweet potatoes, bring back to the boil and cook, covered, for 15–20 minutes until tender.

3. Drain the potatoes well, then cover the pan with a clean tea towel and leave to stand for 2 minutes. Remove the skins and mash with a potato masher until fluffy.

4. Add the reserved butter to the potatoes and stir in evenly. Spoon the mash into a serving dish and serve hot, topped with chunks of parsley butter.

VICHY CARROTS WITH PARSLEY

This dish originates from France and is named after the town of Vichy in the centre of France. To be authentic, the recipe must be made with Vichy mineral water but any other type will be fine too!

SERVES: 4-6

PREP TIME: 10-15 MINS

COOK TIME: 10-15 MINS

INGREDIENTS

2 tbsp unsalted butter

450 g/1 lb carrots, cut into 5-mm/¼-inch slices

1 tbsp sugar

bottle of Vichy mineral water

salt and pepper

2 tbsp chopped fresh flat-leaf parsley

1. Melt the butter in a large, heavy-based saucepan over a medium–high heat. Stir in the carrots, then stir in the sugar and season with salt and pepper to taste.

2. Pour over enough Vichy water to cover the carrots by 5 cm/2 inches and bring to the boil. Reduce the heat to medium and leave the carrots to simmer, uncovered, stirring occasionally, until they are tender, all the liquid has been absorbed and they are coated in a thin glaze.

3. Adjust the seasoning if necessary, transfer to a serving dish and stir in the parsley. Serve immediately.

DRESSED BEETROOT SALAD

SERVES: 4-6

PREP TIME: 20 MINS PLUS CHILLING

COOK TIME: 25-40 MINS

INGREDIENTS

900 g/2 lb raw beetroots

4 tbsp extra virgin olive oil

1½ tbsp red wine vinegar

2 garlic cloves, finely chopped

2 spring onions, very finely chopped

salt

1. Carefully remove the roots from the beetroots without cutting into the skin, then cut off all but 2.5 cm/1 inch of the stalks. Gently rub the beetroots under cold running water, without splitting the skins, to remove any dirt.

2. Put the beetroots in a saucepan with water to cover and bring to the boil. Cover, reduce the heat slightly and cook for 25–40 minutes, depending on the size, until the largest beetroot is tender when pierced with a skewer or knife.

3. Meanwhile, put the oil, vinegar, garlic, spring onions and salt to taste in a jar with a screw-top lid and shake until emulsified, then set aside.

4. Drain the beetroots and rinse under cold running water until cool enough to handle, then peel away the skins. Thickly chop or slice the beetroots, then put in a bowl and pour over the dressing. Cover and chill in the refrigerator for at least 1 hour.

5. To serve, gently toss the salad and transfer to a serving bowl.

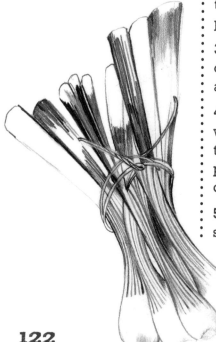

ROASTED CARROT DIP WITH FETA

The bright orange colour of carrots signifies their high beta and alpha carotene levels. This gives them the ability to rejuvenate your skin and other organs.

SERVES: 4-6   **PREP TIME: 15 MINS**   **COOK TIME: 40 MINS**

INGREDIENTS

500 g/1 lb 2 oz carrots, thickly sliced

100 ml/3½ fl oz extra virgin olive oil

2 tsp cumin seeds, toasted and ground

115 g/4 oz feta cheese (drained weight) or fresh firm goat's cheese, crumbled

salt and pepper

1 small bunch of fresh coriander, finely chopped, to garnish

1. Preheat the oven to 200°C/400°F/Gas Mark 6. Put the carrots in an ovenproof dish, pour over the oil and cover the dish with foil. Bake in the preheated oven for about 25 minutes.

2. Meanwhile, heat a dry, heavy-based frying pan over a medium–high heat. Add the cumin seeds and cook for 3–4 minutes, tossing the seeds frequently, until lightly toasted and fragrant. Leave to cool, then grind using a pestle and mortar or an electric grinder, to form a coarse powder.

3. Remove the foil from the ovenproof dish, toss in the ground cumin seeds and bake for a further 15 minutes, or until tender.

4. Mash the carrots with a fork, combining them with the oil in the dish, or whizz them to a paste in a blender or food processor. Season to taste with salt and pepper and spoon into a serving dish. Scatter the crumbled feta cheese over the top and garnish with the coriander. Serve warm or at room temperature.

BEETROOT & CHICKPEA HUMMUS

This is a great twist on the traditional hummus, with the vibrant red and tangy flavour of the beetroot really adding visual impact and a fuller flavour.

SERVES: 4-6   **PREP TIME: 10 MINS**   **COOK TIME: NONE**

INGREDIENTS

400 g/14 oz canned chickpeas, drained and rinsed
1 garlic clove, roughly chopped
100 g/3½ oz cooked beetroot
1½ tbsp tahini
juice of ½ lemon
3 tbsp olive oil
salt and pepper
vegetable crudités, to serve

1. Place the chickpeas, garlic and beetroot in a food processor or blender and process until broken into crumbs.

2. Add the tahini and lemon juice and process again, pouring in the olive oil until the hummus is the consistency you like. Season to taste with salt and pepper.

3. Serve the hummus with vegetable crudités.

HERO TIPS

The dark-green, purple-tinged leaves of the beetroot are an edible vegetable too and can be sliced or steamed. Like the root, they are rich in vitamins, minerals and carotenes.

INDEX